# THE CHOICES

NORMAN THOMAS

# the
# CHOICES

IVES WASHBURN, INC. · NEW YORK

THE CHOICES

# CONTENTS

# PROLOGUE:
# THE CHOICES

It had been suggested to me that I write a short book for younger readers, summing up my ideas about the problems of today. However, as I progressed with the writing of the book, I realized the complexity of these problems required treatment more suited to adults with the hope that some young people would also find it of interest.

I had been speaking in colleges before my recent illness under the title, *What Are the Answers?*, dealing especially with the war in Vietnam, the race conflict in the United States, and the general problem of poverty. I thought that these problems were interrelated and developed my speeches accordingly, noting that as a whole they would provide much more specific answers than I could give in one speech. This is true even in a short book.

But there were some things I thought I could discuss with some assurance more briefly. I believe that we can and must bring an end to all war in a thermonuclear age; I believe that we can and must achieve racial harmony, and I believe that central to the solution of these problems is the achievement, in an economy of abundance, of an end to the bitter poverty which disgraces so much of the earth.

Absolutely essential if we are to do anything in these areas is the dethronement of what has nearly become an apotheosis of violence. Though I could not give specific answers to some of these questions, I could point out directions we should take; I could offer alternatives. I could provide *some choices*.

I made my first important political speech to a large audience in Madison Square Garden in 1917, in support of Morris Hillquit, the very able Socialist Party candidate for Mayor of New York. The meeting dealt largely with the First World War, our entrance into which the Socialists had opposed. To fashion a world without war seemed to me a primary concern. I also believed that to attain peace, the world would have to concern itself with creating a world in which social justice prevails.

Almost fifty years from that day, I made what turned out to be my last speech in November of 1967. I spoke before a large audience of labor leaders in Chicago. Once again, the subject was peace. After fifty tumultuous years, years which saw victory for what was the better side in two world wars, the United States was involved in a very cruel war in Vietnam, and living under the constant threat of a third world war.

In spite of, or because of, some of the important changes of the years, our world is caught up in revolutionary ferment, is engaged in a feverish search for answers—just as we were fifty years ago. I write this book with the very real fear that we do not have another fifty years.

Of course I realize that the scope of our problems is very broad: it covers changing concepts in religion, the educational process, sexual mores, the concept of the family, the new art and its significance, and the spiritual and economic effects of an increasingly pervasive cybernetics. When I spoke, I alluded to the latter subjects, but I did not discuss them in depth, and I shall do the same in this short book, merely stating that they contribute greatly to the convulsive character of our times.

One thing I am convinced of is the lack of any absolute solutions in books which give us the wisdom of our ancestors. Though these books are important for a picture of origins, I cannot recommend any book written before the Second World War as adequate to meet the problems of our complex times, or even to give an entirely accurate discussion of modern socialism, capitalism, communism or nihilism. Above all, we must seek for intelligent answers to our difficulties. I reject the idea that the incalculable destruction created by violent revolution will bring a desirable answer to the problems of war and peace.

I ask you not to judge *The Choices* as to whether it is basically optimistic or pessimistic but, rather, as to the value of my suggestions. I am very critical of what is now called the Establishment in Washington, Moscow, or Peking, but I have great affection for my own country, and confidence—especially within the oncoming generation —in its salvation. To use symbolic terms, I am one of those who desire to wash the flag, not burn it.

I recognize that washing the flag requires more than political or economic group action. It requires personal action, *your* action in the ending of violence, the achievement of fraternity and honesty.

I wrote this book before the national elections on November 5, 1968, and I shall be able to refer to their results only briefly. But I have been more interested, in any case, in the issues I have discussed, none of which will be solved in 1969 by the major party candidates.

I could not have finished the book at all had not my friend and former secretary, Timothy Sullivan, been able to be with me during much of its writing. I also wish to thank my daughter, Frances Gates, who helped me in the writing of the early versions of the book. I also owe great thanks to my editor, Bettina Peterson.

November, 1968

# 1

## WE MUST CHOOSE PEACE

Many people ask, "Can we have a world without war?" If the answer is "No," we shall have no world at all, certainly not a decent world in which we would want to live. War is one of the oldest of human institutions, and in the past, it has cursed mankind without destroying it. But now in the age of thermonuclear weapons, the literal power of destruction has been acknowledged by every American President, the rulers of Russia, and almost all other competent observers. We cannot waste time in finding alternatives to war. The Hebrew prophets wrote eloquently of a time when "Men should beat their swords into plowshares and their spears into pruning hooks." That hope has been an inspiration to men down through the ages, but how inadequate that process would be in the age of guided missiles!

We are sometimes told that the very danger inherent in missiles aids the cause of peace. It may be true that if it had not been for fear of hydrogen bombs, the United States and Russia would have started World War III, but it is ridiculous to think that these nations and others that spend billions of dollars on modern weapons will always refrain from using them in a war because of their catastrophic danger. Familiarity breeds contempt, and no formal or informal agreement will prevent the outbreak of a war by accident or passion, or the disastrous confidence of one side or another in immediate victory. I have often written and said that if flying saucers have come near enough to the United States or Russia to land, they have not done so because the commander has said "Home, James! This madness may be catching." For, if we are to regard ourselves as rational animals, it is sheer lunacy to keep on building up a world of anarchic nations at a total cost to mankind of approximately $200 billion annually, while allowing one to exist in which three-quarters of the people live on the threshold, not merely of hunger, but of starvation.

Against this background, peace in Vietnam will be a tremendous asset, but there are many other situations around us which could easily and promptly explode into world war: the Arab nations and Israel; Turkey and Greece over Cyprus; one or more of the African Nations against the imperialist apartheid in South Africa; India against Pakistan; and imperialism in Portuguese territories. Years of experience have taught us that these crises will not be settled by eloquent orations on peace.

Many of us hoped, too confidently, that fear and horror at the potential of the bomb, and the experience of the general agonies of World War II, would lead men to take long strides toward building a world without war, but the steps that have been taken were very much shorter and

weaker than we had hoped. Among them is the United
Nations, valuable though inadequate to its task, a situation that is exacerbated by the American policy of ex-
cluding Red China, the most populous nation in the world.
However, the work of the United Nations has been valuable enough to give us greater hope of achieving a world
without war by improving it than by making the new start
some voices are urging.

After World War II, there was some conflict among
peace seekers between the advocates of total disarmament
and those of dependence on the United Nations. Most of
them, however, recognized that the two things should go
together. We need disarmament under the control that
only an international organization can handle.

I have steadily advocated that war could only be gotten
rid of by imposing total disarmament down to a police
level, under the supervision and enforcement of a United
Nations developed along the lines of the well-known
book, *World Peace Through World Law* by Grenville
Clark and Louis Sohn, and their subsequent writing. The
active expression of the ethical truth that above all nations
exists humanity, should be accompanied by leadership of
the United Nations in a cooperative form of economic aid
to economically underdeveloped areas. That is a way to
break the neo-imperialism that is now appearing. The cooperative aid of all nations to members of the group that
need special help is likely to be intellectually and emo-
tionally far more satisfactory than the aid given by com-
peting rich uncles to dependent nephews. All of this requires an end of the effort by any single power to police
the world or any considerable part of it. Neither the

United States, nor any other powerful nation has enough wisdom or strength to play policeman to the rest of mankind.

Logic and history unite to show us that world peace cannot be so simply won and maintained. We did not so nearly displace internal strife within nations with law by making all individuals pacifists. We shall not get or maintain the disarmament of modern states by making them pacifists, immensely desirable as that would be. We must have an alternative to war in the dealing of nations with each other, just as individuals have within nations. Nevertheless, the struggle for disarmament is extraordinarily important. Disarmament on the long Canadian border was a principal factor in keeping the peace in the 19th century, when peace was menaced by boundary disputes in the Northeast and Northwest. The War of 1812, which neither side won, led to agreement between the United States and Britain, at that time sovereign over Canada, and was a great achievement. Moreover, the emotional pressure necessary to make nations support the terrible expense of a modern arms race, is itself an important factor in the building of tensions from which wars may spring.

An adequate United Nations requires disarmed, not armed nations, and it must have its own police forces, loyal to it rather than to individual nations, much as the United States Army is loyal to the United States rather than to the individual states.

Perhaps the greatest difficulty will be to insure that individual nations give up acting as guardians of right and justice throughout the world. This general principle is

very ably discussed in Senator Fulbright's *The Arrogance
of Power*. There is a lot of conscious hypocrisy in America
in the belief that our democracy must be ready to defend
any small nation against every form of social revolution
that might spring up or attack it from the outside, the
devil always being communism. That will only lead to a
prolonged repetition of the tragic struggle in Vietnam.

Our State Department says we have treaties with forty-
two nations that it believes may compel us to give active
military aid! This is a doctrine that really denotes a strong
assertion of the "arrogance of power." Some leftists go
quite as far as any rightist in maintaining that it is impossible to have a world without war, unless and until
there are common beliefs in politics and economics. Such
universal ideologies, if they were of the right sort, would
doubtless be a blessing for mankind, but their mere philo-
sophic espousal would not prevent wars. Christianity,
Islam, and Communism bear this out. Men are not content
with a general similarity of ideology. In the churches and
in the now much-divided Communist Party, this is evident.
Each group of true believers has found it harder to tolerate heretics than open enemies. Some of the cruelest
wars of history were fought under the banner of the cross,
and common reference for Marxist-Leninism has by no
means superseded national interest or prevented serious
disagreement on what may be called theological interpretation. This is the basis of the present clash between Russia and China, and the growing rejection in the satellite
states of a binding Russian version of Marxism in action.
At this moment probably the strongest ideology in the
world today is nationalism. Under its emotional and prac-

tical pressure, nineteenth century imperialism has been all but destroyed. There is a sense in which nationalism has been responsible for certain kinds of liberty and an interesting variety in cultures. But militaristic, nationalist states have been quite amoral. Each has acted as a god, in whose service any lie, deceit, or brutality is justified, and disobedience to its orders to kill has counted as among the worst of crimes.

This atmosphere is not favorable to the sort of program necessary to bring about a world without war. As it is we shall have to deal with the present crises on less than ideal terms, but we cannot even begin unless the temporary steps we take are in the direction of the world reorganization I have outlined, and are partly inspired by the possibility of its ultimate success.

I. F. Stone, in his weekly, after the short Israeli-Arab war of June, 1967, wrote an eloquent article on reconciliation, which is indeed the basis for the world we hope for. The article was not well-received by those to whom it was addressed, but that it was written at all and aroused as much interest as it did is a hopeful sign.

There are many voices that claim there will always be wars. They say that some of man's finest characteristics and actions have been connected with war; that our chief heroes have been war heroes, in whose honor the greatest songs and poems have been written. The human species has the instinct for aggression inherent in the evolutionary process. It not only developed the species, but was able to make it the most dangerous form of animal life. It is true that aggression is a primary instinct that makes war possible, but does not make it inevitable (see Dr. Konrad

Lorenz's recent book, *On Aggression*). Nor is it true that our cultural history of acceptance and glorification of war, has made extreme violence a part of our way of life. Depressing as the outlook is, it is encouraging that there is so much discussion of disarmament and peace, and that there are the beginnings of an organization, such as the United Nations, dedicated to a world without war.

Men have remained aggressive, but they have by no means always expressed their aggressions as did their forefathers. We no longer fight wars in the spirit of, let us say, the Iliad and the Odyssey, and when I consider history, I find encouragement in the fact that the Vikings, so long the war-like ravagers of Western Europe, were the ancestors of the same Scandinavians who today have come nearest to developing governments and institutions devoted to peace, not war. The task of achieving disarmament under responsible control and establishing the principle of the force of law rather than of war is immensely difficult, but evolution and history do not indicate it is impossible.

Still it will be impossible unless we can work out co-existence with communist states. Developments in Russia and her satellites suggest that this is an attainable goal. The importance of having peace gives us a tremendous common interest, and there *has* been a genuine evolution toward peace.

It is far more possible than it seemed in Stalin's time to deal with communists in power. Much of the best-informed opinion today pretty well eliminates communism, per se, as a major threat to peace. It points out that it is itself a divided force, that it has proved capable of some degree of internal reform, and of recognizing individual rights. On the other hand, we have a tendency to declare any movement toward social revolution "communist." This is particularly true of Latin America. There is no doubt that our propaganda equating "freedom" simply with anti-communism is false, and it is often a virtuous rationalization of our own special interests.

This judgment of the world crisis is true and important, but we would be unrealistic if we consider communism too negligible a factor, or easily suited to peace. We shall not succeed in achieving peace, nor shall we deserve to succeed, if we forget communism's denials of individual liberty, and the aggressiveness of its search for power. It is not devoted to pacifism.

It is to the overriding necessity for peace we must appeal. Our great weapon against communism, when it is in the wrong, is to demonstrate the superiority of a democracy that we too often talk about rather than practice.

I repeat the methods by which I believe we can establish peace, or at least bring about the absence of war. They are: universal disarmament down to a police level; the effective control of disarmament through the United Nations, which must increasingly provide more effective alternatives to war through the principle of law; the general abandonment of the idea that a very strong power must assume the role of world policemen, a role for which no nation has the wisdom or the power; the cooperation of all the nations and peoples of the world in the fight against bitter poverty, epidemic disease, and illiteracy. All of these things must be based upon and supported by a general ideal of fraternity to which each nation may make its own particular contribution.

# 2

## RACIAL WAR

## OR RACIAL FRATERNITY?

In 1948, at the time of the political conventions, the
United States seemed to be the strongest and the most
secure nation in the world. The country showed some
tendency to deal realistically with its own problems, for
example, with civil rights. This tendency was notably expressed in a resolution offered by the then Mayor of
Minneapolis, Hubert Humphrey, at the Democratic nominating convention of 1948. To the surprise even of lib-
erals, Humphrey's resolution passed, and he was sent that
fall to the United States Senate where he became a kind
of mouthpiece for opponents of war, and for friends of
integration.

But in the spring of 1968, whole blocks of our capital
city, Washington, were burned. Black smoke hung over
the city, and the burning was accompanied by looting and
vandalism. The President of the United States called up
12,000 troops to protect the city. Washington was only one
of the cities with civil disorder. The assassination of Mar-

tin Luther King, Jr., in the spring of 1968 in Memphis, Tennessee, was followed by rioting of greater or lesser extent in 125 American cities, with an estimated millions in damage.

In the United States and all over the world, men of good will not given to rash judgments or flamboyant statement were speculating publicly about the literal survival of the United States. The very underpinnings of this country seemed in danger of collapse.

We try to reassure ourselves by seeing these riots as somewhat different from the worst summer riots of the preceding four years. The 1968 riots were considered to be the work of a small minority of a minority. Probably so. But bad as they were, they were only a foretaste of the catastrophe a minority of a minority could bring about in modern cities. The 1968 outbreak of violence was accompanied by a monumental outpouring of grief for the slain chief prophet and exponent of nonviolence, whose nonviolence was directed toward a justice for the Negro that rioting can never win. Vice President Humphrey, sponsor of the best resolution on civil rights that has ever been accepted by a major party in this country, had become, officially, a hawk in support of the undeclared war in Vietnam. The war, spiritually and practically, made progress in meeting the needs of the poor impossible, and especially the Negro poor.

How did all this come about? What hopes do we have for solving the race problem, which, as the President's Commission on Civil Disorders has reported, is driving America into two nations—black and white, separate but unequal? How will the American people prevent this? To give even a tentative answer to these vital questions requires a brief review of history.

In some important respects, our country, which we love, has had a Dr. Jekyll and Mr. Hyde policy. One illustration will suffice: The great men who wrote the Declaration of Independence declared that "all men are created free and equal and entitled to life, liberty, and the pursuit of happiness." Their definition of freedom and equality was plain hypocrisy. The men whom they declared free and equal were only the whites. At their hands and those of their successors, the Declaration had no meaning for the Indians, whom they displaced by a series of broken treaties; for the Negroes, who were slaves when the Declaration of Independence was written and for a long time afterwards; and for the Japanese and the Japanese-Americans, whom the President put in concentration camps in 1942, without trial or hearing. Only in the United States was the end of the horrible institution of chattel slavery brought about by a War in which 600,000 of our best youth perished, leaving a race problem still to be solved. At least today we have been brought face to face with it.

The so-called Reconstruction period, which was ended by the compromise under which Rutherford B. Hayes became President in 1877, does not make a handsome story. The triumphant Northern states gave political rights to the Negroes in the defeated South, but they did not provide a well-thought-out economic or political program either for the Negroes or the whites. The Negroes were supposed to carry on, taking their place as citizens, although the majority of them had had no training except as field hands, and were generally brought up with far less care than good farmers gave to their horses and mules. They had been torn completely out of their African tradition, and were not allowed to participate in the American kind of family life. Any member of the family was subject to sale like livestock. Negro women had no defense against the sexual longings of their masters, and the situation after emancipation was not much better. White man's rape was practically never punished, although Negroes guilty of a similar offense against whites were subject to death, legally or by lynching. The white men who were so sure whites were a superior race, insisted that the smallest mixture of Negro blood in men or women made them Negro. There are comparatively few full-blooded Negroes in the United States, and for that white men are chiefly responsible.

The brutal, bigoted Ku Klux Klan that originated in Reconstruction days, largely disappeared when that period ended until it was revived more actively around the turn of the century. Whites and Negroes in the South, as well as in the North, were separated in their churches and schools and in the armed forces of the United States. The separate but equal doctrine as applied to public education was a hypocritical farce.

With this century came the big surge of Negroes into the North and into industry. It was speeded by two World Wars and by the mechanization of the cotton fields. Labor unions, which had their own troubles in these times, were about as Jim Crow as were the churches. Theodore Roosevelt raised a serious political storm by inviting the very moderate Negro leader, Booker T. Washington, to the

White House to lunch. During the First World War, the landlord of my office building in New York City ordered us to discharge a Negro office worker for no reason at all except his color. We finally had to move from that building. The First and Second World Wars necessarily gave Negroes more job opportunities that did not survive the wars in full force, so that after the Second World War, even though there was some improvement in the public attitude, the overall number of Negroes employed in most parts of the United States declined.

Of course there were men, white and colored, who recognized the dangerous lack of humanity in the situation, but they made slow progress until the National Association for the Advancement of Colored People began a very well-planned legal attack based on the Constitution against all sorts of discrimination practiced against Negroes by law and custom. Minor victories in the courts—for instance, the decision knocking out the exclusive white primary in the state of Texas, and the end of the color line in the Army—tended to arouse the public, colored and white, but obviously were not enough to satisfy growing Negro unrest. The great legal victory came in 1954, when the Supreme Court school decision, reversing past decisions, declared it unconstitutional to discriminate against Negroes by a separation which did not and could not justify the description "separate but equal." However, the decision was very far from being easily and automatically applied. The next landmark victory was won by a Negro boycott of the Montgomery, Alabama, bus service. The leader was an eloquent colored clergyman named Martin Luther King. What made it doubly interesting was that it was won on Gandhi's principle of non-violence. This principle of non-violent resistance was used by a group of Negro students who staged a sit-in strike in a Greensboro, North Carolina, restaurant in 1960.

The idea was contagious. It is hardly necessary to tell the story of the Freedom Bus Riders, and of those who opposed social discrimination in which the protesters were often the victims but not the ones who started violence that usually went unpunished. Remember the three martyrs of Philadelphia, Mississippi: Andrew Goodman, Michael Schwerner, and James Chaney; the murder of children in Birmingham, Alabama, by a bomb thrown into a Sunday School room; and the long struggle of James Meredith and others to get into previously all white universities.

Some of the many efforts to break down restrictions by law and custom on the right of Negroes to vote, resulted in legislation to guarantee equality of rights for Americans all over the country. Progress was slower than it ought to have been, but there was progress. Besides the Supreme Court decision of 1954, a Negro leader was enabled for the first time in 1968, largely with Negro votes, to lead the field in a congressional race in Mississippi. Charles Evers was defeated in the run-off by a coalition against him, but what happened was one of the more remarkable of many remarkable gains. Equality of rights and integration were the main goals of Evers' campaign.

These ideas were dramatically expressed in the great Washington March of August, 1963. That was one of the happiest days of my political life. It looked as if we were inaugurating a unique event in history—a non-violent, revolutionary effort toward integration and brotherhood. The spirit of friendship between whites and Negroes, including the police, was something I had never seen. Alas, I have not seen it since, partly because Congress was so slow in adopting the sweeping legislation for equal rights that it has finally passed.

Since that March on Washington, the situation has greatly changed. Disappointed by the slowness of results and angered by white violence, many of the most active Negroes have demanded a change in tactics. For instance, the Student Nonviolent Coordinating Committee, by the early part of 1968, had become the chief advocate of violence. Many of the Negroes and some of their white friends have made a kind of bible out of Franz Fanon's book, *The Wretched of the Earth,* with an introduction by Jean-Paul Sartre. This book is not only a justification of violence in Algeria, but a kind of glorification of anti-colonial wars. There is open talk of guerrilla war in America by an important element in our Negro population.

1967 saw serious riots in many American cities. The President's Commission on Civil Disorders, a very good group, headed by Governor Otto Kerner of Illinois as Chairman, and Mayor John Lindsay of New York as Vice-Chairman, brought in a unanimous report. They found there was no coordination of these riots, that each one was triggered by an event in its own locality, but they foreshadowed more riots, more warfare in our streets, and the impossible and undesirable development of virtually two nations in the United States, separate but unequal. The Commission made sweeping suggestions for action, public and private, to stop this kind of struggle.

This whole development and what lies behind it, has been described and explained with uncommon insight and candor by a great many writers, white and colored, as well as by the President's Commission. We can no longer say we cannot stop possible disasters because of lack of knowledge. Our lack is rather of will and social arrangement.

# 3

# TOWARD RACIAL FRATERNITY

It is easier to outline the problems of racism in America than it is to give the answers to them. Before I begin, may I say I find it encouraging that they are so earnestly and intelligently discussed today by a great many whites and blacks. Indeed, the problem would not be so difficult to solve if the American mind and conscience had awakened in a similar manner in the years between the Emancipation Proclamation and the Supreme Court decision in 1954 on school integration.

It is generally agreed that any practical solution to our racial trouble must stem from a successful war against poverty: that is, to clean up our urban and rural slums, to provide jobs and training for jobs to all who need them, and to improve the quality of all education, especially in the ghettos and the poverty-stricken countryside.

It is as clear as daylight that our goal will not be accomplished without the determination to (1) tackle the whole problem of war which consumes money and ideals so desperately needed at home, and to (2) launch an all-inclusive attack on poverty. We cannot cure Negro poverty and slum conditions without using the same means that are needed to cure all poverty in this rich United States. These facts are generally recognized by the men and organizations concerned with the problems of education, employment, and housing. One of the best of the comprehensive proposals, prepared by that admirable civil-rights organization, the A. P. Randolph Institute, is the *Freedom Budget*. The makers of the *Freedom Budget* believe we are rich enough to be able to afford both guns and butter, but, alas, the government has so far given greater priority to guns.

For instance, President Johnson, who talked a great deal about his desire to finance both the war in Vietnam and a war against poverty in this country, accepted extensive budget cuts in what never were adequately financed programs. Congress did worse: for example, it cut a good program like the Head Start Project as well as food distribution to the poor, and job training programs. All of this happened in the face of reports of starving children in Mississippi and other states, and an infant mortality rate five times higher among Negroes than whites. But if there had to be a choice, the President and the Congress —and a large proportion of the American people—believed that we must tax ourselves to literally destroy Vietnam, rather than to feed our hungry children adequately.

In discussing some of these matters in *Newsweek* in the spring of 1968, Walter Lippmann reached the conclusion that even if we achieved the essential end of the war, our affluent American society would not have the altruism and good sense to implement the recommendations of the President's Advisory Committee on Civil Disorders or the *Freedom Budget*. It is, at this time, not so much new laws that we need, important as they have been and are, but an awakening of our own wills and consciences. Mr. Lippmann did not think that that would happen easily or promptly. Still he felt that it is at least encouraging that an official American commission reported so candidly to the President without justifying the status quo, or appealing to the racist temper of the times by an impassioned denunciation of Negroes because of recent riots.

Our ultimate answer to the problems of racism lies in the hearts of blacks and whites. No law can take care of this, but good laws, of which we now have many, are important not only for the action they call for but for their role in educating us. I remember an informal speech by a Southern civil rights worker who told us how hard it had been for him to sit at a dining table with blacks, but how it soon became a matter of course to deal with them individually and collectively as he would deal with a similar number of his own race. This sort of reaction will automatically help us to answer some of the pressing problems—about housing, for example—which now seem so difficult.

By way of action, I believe that we shall have to accept a program such as that outlined by the *Freedom Budget,* and work for its immediate implementation. Given the condition of the American mood, I know that we shall not be able to implement it all at once, but we cannot sorrowfully relegate its programs to the realm of "mere" Utopian thinking. The *Freedom Budget* proposals have been drawn up by, among others, Leon Keyserling, who was President Truman's top economic advisor. They argue effectively that a long range plan to abolish poverty in the United States could be financed out of the increase in the Gross National Product which the Budget program will almost automatically bring about. Whether this is so or not, we must not accept the idea that its program cannot or will not be financed by the American people.

It is true that programs advocated by the hardheaded men on the President's Advisory Commission on Civil Disorders and from the A. Philip Randolph Institute will not be immediately started—even with the best will in the world. It is, therefore, particularly important for our cities to do what they can immediately in other than strictly economic fields. Thus, they can provide better facilities for recreation in the ghettos, and encourage self-help projects by individuals in the cities and countryside. The efforts of Mayor Lindsay in New York, to give a good example of what can be done, to encourage individual dignity and self-respect along with pride in the city, have a very real value. Programs in a *safe* Central Park, and better lighting on certain streets may actually be more important in averting violence than largely theoretical, grandiose schemes.

I do not think that violence is inevitable, and it is here that some discussion of "Black Power," "Black Nationalism," and "Black Separatism" may be in order. No white man, knowing the history of his own race and the ways it has used violence in its struggles for power or justice, can entirely blame these movements if justice is thought of as an "eye for an eye, and a tooth for a tooth." Actually, whites can have little to say against the blacks, who, in the name of "Black Power," seek a separate nation or at least a wide segregation. But the violence at least implied, or verbally advocated, amounting to attempted guerrilla war in the streets of our cities, such as the kind that broke out upon the assassination of Dr. King, is horrible to contemplate.

The great evil of *apartheid* in South Africa lies in the idea that in our interdependent world each race somehow can be herded into its own corner while the well-being of all is advanced. Thus, black apartheid anywhere, however understandable in view of the past conduct of whites, is a tremendous step away from the vision of those who worked (and died) for integration.

The martyred Martin Luther King Jr.'s eloquent statements about future integration in his "I have a dream" speech are truly inspiring.

Integration of the right sort never intended a dead level of conformity of cultures among American groups. All racial groups can and should make unique contributions to life on this small interrelated planet. However, the contributions of Negroes often sold into slavery by their own chiefs, and held for centuries as such in the American system—cannot be solely determined by their African heritage. In spite of their oppression in this country, they have made a notable contribution to life here especially in music and sports where there was and is less resistance on the basis of color. They have contributed much economically and politically, certainly much more than most school book histories give them credit for, and a realistic revision of these books is in order.

There is a sense in which "Black Power" is a necessity in any true integration. But that does not mean either the impossible task of separating blacks and whites into distinct nations within our borders, nor does it mean that a healthy society could be created on the principle that blacks should vote for blacks and whites for whites.

The idea of a "separate but equal" society held by some Black Power leaders is, I think, even more impractical and harmful than the same doctrine that has been in effect for so many years in Southern schools, and, in a de facto way, in Northern schools. It is opposition to this doctrine that inspired some of the most heroic actions by Negroes and whites who eventually did win the legal abolition of the principle. They were prompted not only by the immorality of "separate but equal" in their educational systems, but by its utter hypocrisy—even if it may have been well intended. It was a principle that corrupted the education of whites as well as Negroes, and this will be its effect on other areas of life if it is extended to them in reverse.

No minority, however conscious of its own identity, scattered throughout the United States, and dependent upon the general economy, can achieve the human values it seeks through the politics of separation. True, minorities can keep pride in their own race much as the Irish and the Jews have done. Even more important, the development of this self-respect and pride in race within a reasonably integrated America can be more successful than attempting extreme separatism that would lead to bloodshed and racial pride which could easily deteriorate into another form of racism to curse the earth.

It is a very serious fact, emphasized by the President's Advisory Commission on Civil Disorders, that many militant Negroes are talking of bringing guerrilla war to city streets. If they do this, they will violate one of the warnings of Dr. Franz Fanon.

He explicitly urged an oppressed minority not to use the sort of guerrilla warfare he had advocated in Algeria. Though this kind of fighting was perhaps a prime factor in the achievement of independence in Algeria, it left no residue of fraternity and nobility of spirit behind it. I think that the future of the world depends upon our ability to find substitutes for violence in human relations.

I acknowledge with real shame that we have not moved faster, and with greater sincerity, to implement the good legislation that has been adopted, and gone ahead with practical plans in the fields of education, housing, and employment where so much needs to be done. But I confess to a certain surprise that some people, many of whom sacrificed greatly to win civil rights, can dismiss what has been achieved as if it had been of no value at all.

With my own eyes I saw what it was like to attempt to register and vote in Mississippi in 1963 if your skin was black. The situation is still bad, but Charles Evers is proof of how much improvement there has been—even in Mississippi—since then. Other Negroes have been elected to responsible posts in the South, and in the North, where Negroes had the legal right to vote, a Carl Stokes has been elected Mayor of Cleveland and a Richard Hatcher has been elected Mayor of Gary, Indiana. The President of the United States has appointed Negroes to important posts. Thurgood Marshall, who, as a lawyer for the NAACP won so many legal battles, is now a member of the Supreme Court. Edward Brooke is a United States Senator from Massachusetts. Robert Weaver was a member of the Cabinet. And there are a number of others that could be mentioned.

These facts are sometimes rejected as nothing but "tokenism." They are more, and even as tokens, they are valuable.

One of the crimes of the whites has been their treatment of Negroes as second class citizens, not entitled, for example, to enter the same factory doors, to sit in the same restaurants, to ride on buses where they please, to live where they choose. The legal acquisition of these rights and their increasing exercise should prove enormously helpful in building self-confidence and stimulating Negroes to those further efforts that are so necessary to the life of America. Racism in the United States threatens the very life of our country, but the one fatal error will be to despair of victory in eliminating it. Every one of us can help the situation by banishing racial hatred from our hearts and deeds.

# 4

## ECONOMICS I:
## ECONOMIC JUSTICE

If I had been told as a boy of all the technological
wonders to come in my lifetime, I might have thought that
by 1969 there would be dancing in the streets in honor
of the achievements of man. But there is no dancing in
the streets today. Everywhere, there is a kind of miasma
in public life, and a desire to return to a "simpler," more
"ideal" way of existence, a life illustrated perhaps, by the
reconstructed 19th century village of Cooperstown, New
York, and its craftsmen.

I must confess that I, too, was charmed when I visited
the village, but I came to myself in time to remember
how little I had liked the tasks that went along with the
"simple life" in the 1880's and 1890's, and the long
hours of the working day. Nostalgia is pleasant, but it often
does not give the true picture.

Certainly, we still have our problems, though it is well
to remember that we have made some progress. But such
social progress as we have made has lagged far behind

our achievements in controlling energy and matter, and what these achievements ideally demand of us in the business of living together. Thousands of young people, everywhere in the world, with some justification are turning away from what they regard as the "Establishment." Nevertheless, in the United States what we call the "welfare state" has remedied many specific wrongs, and made life more tolerable for many citizens.

The glory of the long rise of primitive man is shadowed by the exploitation which has accompanied it. The beginnings of art, architecture, and culture generally, were often financed by the exactions of a ruling class or group from the labor of slaves or people who managed to produce a little more than was necessary simply to sustain life. The ways in which men were exploited by their rulers were various: Prominent among them were the wars so common among tribes, clans, and nations that the rulers always found "legitimate" excuses for "protecting" their society from enemies outside the particular group to which they belonged, and, sometimes, even from enemies within the group.

We have arrived at a tremendous turning point in history. In all the millennia of time men have had to contend with an economy of scarcity. The best of fortune, and the hardest of labor could not provide what might be called an abundance for all, either of things or services. It was not wholly man's hardheartedness or stupidity which verified the scriptural statement that "the poor ye shall always have with you." Incidentally, I have had that verse quoted to me not as statement of fact, but, rather, as a divine denial of any social hope for the poor.

Now we have achieved, at least in some areas of the world, an economy of abundance; to be sure, it is a poorly distributed abundance. So great have been our accomplishments, it is now evident that under proper conditions, our skills and our machinery could conquer the bitter poverty, illiteracy and disease which mar so much of the earth.

As I shall explain, we have by no means used our resources to this end—even in the United States where one-fourth of our citizens live below what is estimated as a proper level of existence. Somehow, the latter fact was brushed under the rug in this country during the decade of the 1950's, and there were many who were inclined, mistakenly, to regard wild luxury and brutal poverty as natural extremes in the generally satisfactory economy of an "affluent society." On a popular level, beginning with the publication of Michael Harrington's *The Other America,* Americans have become more and more aware that we must reconsider that easy reassurance. In the 1960's we have become more conscious of the fact that the obscene problems of poverty, racism, and war are indissolubly connected with our economic problems. An underlying part of this struggle is the nominal attempt to give reality in a democracy to the famous slogan, Liberty, Equality, Fraternity!

As liberty and equality are usually defined, they do not easily travel in double harness. I remember speaking at a certain college, and during the question and answer period a truly aggressive student told me that he hated socialism because it was the enemy of "freedom." After I asked him what he meant, he replied that freedom consisted of the unimpeded right to get rich, to use his ability, no matter what the cost to others, to win advancement.

If that definition were accurate, no decent society should or could tolerate it. In action, it necessarily denies to other people what the "strong man" demands for himself, and justifies as "freedom." On the other hand, the demand for complete equality, requires a pretty high degree of control over social conditions. And that sort of control often seems to require a dictator along the lines of a Bolshevik revolutionary, or his modern successor, Mao Tse-tung. In short, freedom and equality don't automatically live together comfortably. It takes fraternity to make them compatible.

I think that we shall make the fastest progress toward the goal of the possible "good life" for all by realistically looking out at the world and determining what is most demanded by the times. The following approaches seem to me to be imperative:

Enough social control to deal with the pollution of air and water, with the probability of requiring international cooperation in healing what is becoming more and more of a scourge.

Enough social and personal control to check the explosion of population. This danger is, in a way, due to the fruits of our scientific and medical progress. In the past, if our species was to exist at all, there *had* to be a high birthrate because the deathrate was so high. Our society has already conquered much infant mortality, and prolonged average life expectancy. While it varies somewhat, and is not quite as high now as it has been, the uncontrolled birthrate of the human race can breed us to extinction.

Intelligent control over the use of natural resources, and ways to end the destruction of arable land, for instance, by strip mining must be found. We must also begin, in this scientific age, to determine who should own the resources of the earth, both those under and on its surface, and in its waters.

A great many of us were brought up to believe that the "earth is the Lord's, and the fullness thereof," but most of us know that He doesn't collect the rent. The rise in land values since World War II in desirable regions has bestowed fortunes on men for no labor of hands or brain —unless simply hanging on to the land indicates the use of the brain. It is well established that the sale or rental value of the land is determined by social forces. On this point, the former British Prime Minister, Lloyd George, made a very good observation. In urging land reform he argued that a Briton established legal title to his property only by running it back in time to the person who stole it.

Another George, Henry George, believed that a single tax on land would meet all the costs of government and even leave a surplus, besides unburdening labor and capital of taxes on their output. In *Wealth and Poverty,* George makes a strong case against the long historical exploitation of men through the private ownership of land, ownership which may be entirely absentee.

What methods should guide and stimulate the processes of production and distribution? In Western Europe and the United States that question was answered first by feudalism with its enormous socio-economic inequities, and second by a highly competitive, but little controlled economic system, a product of the Industrial Revolution, which began in the latter part of the 18th century. Though it was known as "free enterprise," capitalism bore very heavily on wage workers who had a little more freedom —but often less security—than slaves. I once heard an eminent economist describe the early capitalist system in terms of the old-fashioned steam engine. The search for profit motivated the shovelling in of the coal. The price system acted in much the same manner as the governor on top of the steam engine. Each, as circumstances varied their force, automatically caused a warning to check the "shovelling" from one area to another. I have always felt this to be a good analogy.

The defenders of the free enterprise system, while they confessed that it might not be of the highest quality morally, asserted that, given the nature of man, it was still the best way to achieve a good economy. This opinion it has been rejected in practice by some of its most ardent has been unequivocally refuted in my lifetime. Ironically, proselytizers. It still sounds better to debate the merits of "free enterprise" with, for example, socialism, but actual free enterprise in the older economic sense has become very limited.

Perhaps this can be illustrated by the remarks of an economist who, in my hearing, described the degeneration of free enterprise by saying that the only pure practitioners in the field were small boys playing marbles for keeps. They receive no subsidies such as big farmers get; no tariff preferments; no parity payments like farmers; indeed, they deal in nothing but their marbles.

# 5

# ECONOMICS II:

# THE CHOICE OF MEANS

A great many of the advances in the implementation of the "welfare state" have been accomplished by men who hotly deny the validity of socialism, but who have felt compelled to promote all kinds of measures to, at least, allay poverty, and provide benefits which scarcely justified the theory that "free enterprise" is adequate to meet elemental human needs. As has often been observed, the right of a free man to stay at the Waldorf-Astoria means little to the jobless "free man" on a park bench.

What the welfare state has not done, on the other hand, has been to fully recognize, much less satisfy, the ideals of freedom, equality, or fraternity. It has been able to a certain extent, to silence the cries of the poor by doling out some bread, and, from time to time, even some "cake." We were, for example, finally brought around to the necessity of public housing, but we have never tackled the job of building a city free from the contamination of the ghettos into which poverty has crowded multitudes of

our citizens and thereby destroyed many human values.
Michael Harrington, in *Toward a Democratic Left,* con-
vincingly shows that the very considerable sums spent by
the federal government on housing and highways has
helped the middle-class and the rich far more than the
poor.

The United States, as far back as 1947, recognized by
congressional resolution the duty of the government to
provide full employment. It has also ordained a "minimum
wage" and there is a strong drive to have the state sup-
plement all this by a negative income tax, under which
families will be assured of grants sufficient to bring their
incomes up to a level informed social scientists hold is
necessary for a minimum healthy existence.

In our own restless times, we have to deal with immediate crises in employment, housing, health, and education
at the same time that we consider answers to these crises
in terms of ultimate planning. This planning must have
the general support of the electorate in purpose and in
execution, and one of our main tasks is to win this support. The planning also has to take account of somewhat
unpredictable changes which this age of cybernetics is
bringing us, and will continue to bring us in the next fifty
years.

Furthermore, it has to involve community groups in
some form of what has been called "participatory democracy," which means, among other things, that our
industrial society needs a far better way than has yet been
found to achieve more satisfactory relations between
management, in its broadest sense, and employees.

One example of the problems in this area, of course,

concerns the elemental one of simply working to keep people alive even in America. As I write, there is a notable attempt to fly food and medical supplies to the beleaguered people of Biafra, where children are dying of starvation at a rate that brings into question every assumption of humanity to which the world pretends. But there are children starving in this country, too, where the problem is complicated by white racism, and by the effort to confront a form of black apartheid.

The situation is also made more difficult by the fact that some immediate measures for the amelioration of poverty in this country, which have already received widespread support from both liberal and conservative economists, are anathema to a middle-class America which holds fast to the belief that "he who will not work should not eat," unless, of course, he has plenty of inherited wealth.

Our western industrial civilization has undoubtedly been made possible by a work-oriented society, motivated by a tremendous desire for profit. Nevertheless, when Dr. Milton Friedman of the University of Chicago, in 1964, a leading adviser of Barry Goldwater in his candidacy for the Presidency, proposed the negative income tax I became convinced that it was the best practical idea for the immediate relief of poverty in America, although it doesn't present an ideal picture of our society. The plan is to have a family submit an income tax return with the assurance that the government will provide enough money to persons and families reporting incomes below a certain amount to bring their income up to this level, a sum which is determined by current minimal standards for a decent existence. Theoretically, it would squarely meet the problems of the worst sort of poverty at a cost not too much greater than that of our very unsatisfactory welfare—public-assistance programs.

The latest estimates I have seen (in *The New York Times*) are that federal expenditures for welfare are now at eight billion dollars (1967), a sum which does not reach a large number of the poor in this country at all. The most conservative estimate of what a viable and comprehensive program would cost is eleven billion dollars. However, I agree with those who favor a considerably higher sum, especially as statistics on the number of the poor are outrageously inadequate. For instance, in *The Second Civil War,* by Dr. Garry Wills, a study of riot-torn America, the author states that it is estimated that 25% of the young Negro males in this country were not included in the 1960 census. In Wills' study of the Detroit riot of 1967, he gives sound reasons for his belief that the casualty rate was much higher than the official reports.

The negative income tax is attacked by some opponents as removing a spur to man's willingness to work. It is argued that men will be paid for doing nothing. This argument would have more force if the poor we are talking about were a community of single men with no dependents, single men for whom self-sustaining jobs could be provided, and which they ought to take. However, the crucial fact is that single men comprise barely one-fourth of the people for whom aid ought to be provided. There are also the physical invalids; mothers and their children; the old, and the mentally incompetent.

I do not asume that it is entirely society's fault that men want to avoid work, or that some men would be content to live on government doles, and I wish that I could think of a system less open to criticism than the negative income tax. It will not answer the all-important problem of encouraging men to work in more than a dollar and cents spirit, to work for their own self-respect, to help society, to earn respect from their fellow workers.

It is true that government aid, if it is regarded as sufficient to bring on the good society, will be woefully misspent. Individual motivation must be stressed so far as society can do it. Aid of all sorts must be administered with a minimum of bureaucracy, and a maximum of honesty.

Our present version of the welfare state is vehemently attacked because of over-centralization. What must be done, it is claimed, should come from a reasonable division between federal and other agencies, with far more of the tasks going to the state, local communities, and even non-governmental groups. It is argued that decentralization is necessary if we are to achieve that form of participatory democracy which is now so much in verbal favor.

This argument deserves considerable evaluation. The more society can evoke the participation of Henry Wallace's "common man" in the organization and accomplishment of good housing, education, and employment, the better it is and will be. Nevertheless, considering the prospect of this participation, I am less sanguine than others. Achieving the good that society requires, as nearly as it can be obtained, the equality of right, i.e., the right to vote, speak, or receive social aid, should be the same whether it be in Mississippi or in New York. And this means federal action to bring it about.

In my own experience, the federal bureaucracy is at
least no worse, and in most cases better, than state
bureaucracies, yet in 1968, it is the states that are spend-
ing on a proportionately larger scale than the federal
government. State boundaries, among other things, were
not originally drawn with reference to efficient production.
The economic problems, for instance, are very similar
throughout the urban community which now stretches
from north of Boston to south of Washington, that area
which has been called by Herman Kahn and Anthony
Weiner, "Boswash," and a fair question may be, "What
can decentralization do for us?"

Whatever the answer, there must be federal supervision.
During my life, moreover, every successful social movement has been forced to place its first reliance on some
degree of federal action: Social Security, Medicare, housing
and employment legislation, and the minimum wage. In
some cases the states began work along these lines, but
most states were financially unable to effectively implement them under our present division of taxing powers
and the different economic levels in the states. Anti-child
labor laws, which were a great issue in my younger years,
and about which we thought we would have to have a
constitutional amendment, were finally adopted by the
states, but generally as the result of nationwide agitation.
Some states pioneered in social services and women's
suffrage legislation, but here again the great fight was on
the federal level, and in the latter case a federal constitutional amendment was necessary. Emphatically, it took
federal action in our own time to remove judicial restrictions, whether de jure or de facto, on Negro civil rights.

The list could be prolonged and there is no one easy rule of centralization or decentralization which applies. As in many fields, including education, we have been on our way to a better combination of federal-state action than the present critics of centralization would admit. Our present troubles do concern centralization and decentralization; the latter issue in the educational system involves decentralization from the state to the city to the local school boards. It is an unsolved issue.

While it certainly requires federal action to guarantee anything to all Americans in the way of Social Security or Medicare, it is not centralization of control by the federal government which raises problems in these fields, but the failure of society to make them the blessing they ought to be for the very poor. In a society as rich as ours the right of every person to health services is as valid as that to education. It is very imperfectly granted. It is people like myself who get more effective benefits from Social Security and Medicare than do the poor. It is ridiculous to think that we can be protected, even partially, on a state level for instance in the very important field of drugs. Ideally, as in the case of air and water pollution, we shall need international action to insure:

a) proper prescription of drugs and notice of their dangers and

b) reasonable prices to consumers for these items.

These facts were brought out, among others, in the Kefauver investigation during the fifties and, more recently, in the Senator Gaylord Nelson investigations. However, they have not evoked proper protection of the American consumer by our government, and the international variation is ridiculous. These developments have been noted in various reports, most recently by Morton Mintz in the September '68 issue of the *Progressive*.

The United States should greatly improve its own controls and be active in urging international controls of pharmaceutical drugs, together with other governments. In this field, as in many others, men, women, and children need protection from exploitation, whether they live in America or Afghanistan.

# 6

# ECONOMICS III:
# SOME FURTHER QUESTIONS

In the building of a decent society, the role of labor unions is important. What I have been urging in these chapters will not amount to much unless it is backed by labor. Times have so changed that, under our present collective bargaining arrangements, which are enormously better than those of the fighting days of the 1920's, it is possible for unions, even relatively small unions, to practically close down an industry. For example, a union on a newspaper which represents only a small part of the paper's operation, can call for a strike which will involve every aspect of the printing of the newspaper, because the chief example of fraternity among unions is respect for each other's picket lines.

For most of my lifetime, what it is now fashionable to call the "Establishment" disliked labor unions and particularly strikes. In the 1920's and early 1930's, I was arrested numerous times for arguing for the right of workingmen to organize and bargain collectively for their rights. Work-

ers were at a great disadvantage in the struggle for higher
wages and better working conditions when they had to
face a monopolistic or oligopolistic group of employers
who had the machines and the public organization to
fight divided workers.

But in the 1930's under the New Deal, the right to
organize and to strike was accepted. Some of the wisest
industrialists thought it was worth consenting to that right
as a partial "reward" to workers for not turning to dreaded
communism. It took considerable time before it became
evident what powerful, well-organized workers could ac-
complish in crippling their industries and services. Workers began to protest not only against profit-making organizations, but against industries and services not controlled
by the profit motive that represented the state which, the
workers argued, could find the money for their extremely
legitimate demands.

Not so surprisingly in the United States, many workers
have rejected the idea of the nationalization of the major
industries. I remember the statement of a former member
of the Socialist Party, now an executive of the International Steel Workers Union: "It's easier to strike against
private industry than it is against the 'State'."

In a clear clash of principles, most unions have naturally put their own interests first above any duty they
owe to society for maintaining such vital services as the
police, fire department, publicly owned utilities, etc.
Legislatures have responded in New York and other areas
by outlawing strikes against the state, and by imposing
heavy penalties on strikers. This scheme has not worked
satisfactorily. Often the penalties apply only to the leaders

of strikes, which immediately makes them martyrs in the eyes of their followers. The fact that there is seldom a person to replace the arrested leader, or even more important, a mass of workers to take the place of the strikers, has left the government with a very small club to use against strikes.

These laws, like an early New York law, the Condon-Wadlin Act, were directed only against employees of the state. The resultant confusion in many states led, for example, to a situation in which transportation workers in New York were subject to prohibitions which did not and still do not apply to the great providers of electrical power, where a short suspension of power could cause immense damage, and a long strike, disaster.

Some unions argue that all society has to do is to surrender to their demands in the fields where they have the right and the power to enforce their rules without society's asking for any accounting to the city, state, or nation. As yet this clash between the right to refuse to work on enforced terms, even where the alternative has been to strike and seriously threaten all society, has never been satisfactorily resolved. But very recently, in some of our cities, there have been strikes of policemen and firemen who necessarily have to be beyond strikes if we are to survive.

I confess that I have no answer to these problems in terms of law, although finally the answer to them will have to come from the law. The law will have to recognize the fact that the government cannot interfere in strikes unless there is an immediate threat of disaster. The principle must be based on the needs of society, and not on the very artificial distinction between "private" and "state" ownership. For instance, in my state of New York the Consolidated Edison Company should be governed by the needs of society because of the disasters which even a short strike by that "private concern" could bring. In line with this dictum, of course, there should be a law which holds that "public" employees whether their pay-checks and other benefits come from public or private sources should get at least as good a wage as employees with the right to strike.

The difficulties of which we have been speaking would be obviated, or at least lessened, by some progress in the democratization of unions, as well as by the democratization of the groups which employ unions. This has to mean, especially in the largest firms, representation by workers on the board of directors.

Strikes against great industries like steel, oil, or coal are no longer directed against particular owners—Rockefeller, Carnegie, Frick, etc.—but, rather, are undertaken against the industry as a whole with the idea that the strikers could hardly do worse against the absentee stockholders.

There is still a great need for more thoughtful discussion in this field. Much of that discussion will be critical of the failure of the United States to do more than it has done. But, in all fairness, it must be pointed out that the United States, under internal and external pressures, has made progress since the days when the American Railway Association, a very radical institution in its time, opened its membership to all *white* workers in the industry.

I have not said anything very specific in this chapter

about the agricultural situation and the peculiar exploitation of its large body of migratory labor. All the protections written into law for labor should apply to agricultural workers, and special efforts should be made to let small farmers, sharecroppers, and migrant workers know the very considerable protections they are now afforded by the law, whether they are white or black. In 1963, after a meeting of the group later to become the Mississippi Freedom Democratic Party, which urged the sharecroppers to vote for their own candidate in a special mock election, a sharecropper told me that the reason registration of Negroes in that district was small, was not so much fear of physical retaliation from whites as that of losing their pieces of land. It was becoming steadily easier for white owners to use machinery, rather than depend on the old system of sharecroppers. Thousands have left Mississippi and other Southern states for Northern and Midwestern slums at a time when a government investigation showed that Mississippi children were suffering from malnutrition.

The basic indictment of the economics of agriculture not only here but in the rest of the world, is that it depends on cutting down production to raise prices. It is true farmers are entitled to a better return for their labor but a way must be found in which the demand can be connected with a system which increases production in the United States and other fertile countries but does not exploit the soil. There have been some good official reports on the situation, but most of them have been promptly shelved. It is a great indictment of us all that the ultra-conservative Senator Eastland is paid over $100,000 a year not to grow certain crops, when he is surrounded, even in his own county, by abysmal poverty.

In a certain sense, American agriculture deserves great credit. Farmers, by the intelligent use of machinery, fertilizer, and crop rotation, have so improved production that 6% of them produce 95% of the food. And yet there is hunger even in America.

Part of my answer to the plight of agriculture in America is the position taken by the National Sharecroppers Fund and the Rural Administration Fund. I strongly recommend that interested readers get in touch with these organizations, of which Fay Bennett is the National Secretary. I write this with a sense of shame that I knew so little about rural poverty when I ran for President in 1928 and even in 1932. I barely knew what a sharecropper was, and I should like to record my thanks to H. L. Mitchell for enlisting me as something of a pioneer in the struggle of Arkansas sharecroppers who were being driven off the land. When some of us finally roused the interest of Washington, the best we got was a provision in some of the contracts saying that the great benefits to landowners were to be given on condition that they would keep the same number of tenants (cash-paying tenants), sharecroppers and field hands as they had formerly, insofar as it was consistent with discipline and the interest of the landlords.

Since then, progress has been made. The Mexican-American grape pickers in California have staged a heroic and partially successful struggle for their right to organize. They have been well led by an advocate of non-violent direct action, Cesare Chavez. How slow the progress is may be symbolized by the fact that a small group of share-croppers found their way to the Democratic Convention as long ago as 1936 to explain their plight. And after all these years, the Reverend Ralph Abernathy and his associates in the Southern Christian Leadership Conference sent a mule team, symbolic of their poverty, to the Democratic Administration in Washington during the summer of 1968, and got not very much more helpful publicity than did the group in 1936.

On all of these points—employment, education, and housing—I have been unable to lay down very specific programs because so much expert knowledge is necessary. I have tried to indicate lines of procedure, and I should like to mention again some particular studies: Michael Harrington's invaluable work, *Toward a Democratic Left;* the *Freedom Budget,* plus the *Report of the President's Advisory Commission on Civil Disorders.*

The one absolutely essential thing, as I have said, is planning, planning which takes account of more than the current year. Planners should think in terms of what is necessary to correlate the many activities among federal, state, and local governments. Perhaps more than anything else, planning should be concerned with engaging the participation of the people not only in the passage of good laws, but in protecting them against corruption and in providing types of work in which workers will be more than a hand, a human tool. Too often, this sort of planning is undertaken but never implemented.

Recently, the role of planning has been attacked—and not only by the Hippies. There is even a song which stresses "loving" rather than "planning." It seems to me ridiculous to imply that there is necessarily a contradiction between the emotion of loving, and the intellectual and practical art of making this loving effective.

Economics is not a science like physics. In the last analysis, the answers to these problems must come from a fraternity which is more than a word in a Fourth of July oration.

# 7

# TOWARD CIVIL LIBERTIES
# AND CIVIL RIGHTS

In New Jersey, during a long-drawn-out labor conflict in 1926, I tested the right of the sheriff to enforce indefinitely what he said was his "right" to forbid a meeting of strikers. I was arrested. The policeman who took me for arraignment before a somewhat befuddled Justice of the Peace, said while we waited: "Mr. Thomas, what you was doing was moral all right, but I don't think 'twas legal. Some things is legal that ain't moral, and some things is moral that ain't legal, and what's a poor cop to do about it?"

The policeman's question is still highly pertinent as it applies to the fields of civil liberties and civil rights. The separation of the two categories in my opinion is not sound philosophically. The right to speak, to vote, to sit where you choose on a bus are all expressions of the rights an individual in the United States of 1968 must have if he is to possess the human dignity of a man.

However, it is also true that no decent, orderly society can exist in which there aren't some restraints on personal rights in the interests of fair play among individuals in their roles as neighbors, workers, and citizens. As I have said, freedom and equality are not easily reconciled in every matter. The process requires human attention, and that fact is, to me, an illustration of the difficulties with absolutes. To take two simple examples: No absolute freedom can justify your driving on the wrong side of the road to the peril of your neighbors, and no absolute freedom can deny to society the right to protect itself from dangerous diseases by ordering vaccinations or inoculations. Some people may object to vaccinations on philosophical grounds, but their value to all is so well proven that society is justified, at least under certain circumstances, in requiring them.

The rights of freedom of speech, press, and association have not been, and, I think, ought not to be interpreted so as to forbid any libel laws, or laws against the uninhibited circulation of obvious pornography—however difficult it may be to draw the line. Nor can any society accept as an ordinary right, or ordinary civil liberty, the right to join in an armed attack on City Hall. If such an attack is to be justified, it must be undertaken according to the philosophy of violent revolution.

On the other hand, I do not think that a democracy has any right to forbid the more or less theoretical discussion of issues which may include an advocacy of ultimate violence unless certain things are done. The point is not that such advocacy is, per se, beneficial to society, but, in my judgment, that it is better to deal with the advocates of future violence by argument and demonstration than by police power. I think a careful reading of history proves this point.

It is well to remember that heresy is a growing factor in our society. Without it there would have been no progress. We can risk listening to many extreme opinions, to many false prophets if we have time to answer them by word or deed. These attempts have been historically more successful than police-club repression.

In my lifetime in America we have seen real progress in achieving civil liberties, even if there has not been and perhaps never can be a final victory in this area. There was far more freedom of speech, of the press, and of association during the undeclared war in Vietnam, for example, than in our previous wars. The Vietnam war, however, brought to the forefront issues too long neglected. I refer especially to conscription, particularly conscription for military duty. To make all men subject to the draft is the strongest imaginable assertion of the right of society to equality of service at the expense of the individual—regardless of his own principles. It denies freedom, and does not achieve an equality of burdens. President John F. Kennedy admitted the latter statement, but commented that life itself is unfair.

I suppose that if we were to have wars like those of the past, our nation might assert the right of conscription in order to save its life. But present conditions, which include competitive armaments supplemented by large-scale conscription, more often than not endanger the life of the nation rather than preserve it. Even if I had more faith than I have in the usefulness of war in a thermonuclear age, I must point out that war between atomic powers would probably be over in a matter of hours—before vast conscripted armies could be put to work. Conscription can, and does, give a ruler far too large a force to play with. However you may judge this argument, I am fully persuaded of the value of the campaign to abolish conscription in favor of an all-volunteer army. This position is held by men whose stands on other matters are as far from mine as Senator Goldwater's. It has been well-argued by the small Council For a Volunteer Military [our goal of course is to abolish war], which is based at the University of Chicago, and in which the conservative economist Milton Friedman is the moving spirit.

However one feels about war, there can be no rational denial of the fact that in terms of civil liberties no requirement of government is comparable to conscription in its denial of individual freedom. To a high degree, property is a social arrangement over which the government, as the agent of society, has a right to more control than it does over an individual's life and conduct. War is organized murder, and a man may believe that it is necessary, but for a government to inculcate this doctrine, and to force a man to take an active part in its horrors is the ultimate crime against civil liberties. That is partially recognized by our draft laws, which grant exemption from military service to conscientious objectors to war. But under our present laws, it requires an objection to *all* wars, although it is just as much of a violation of a man's person and personality to force him, against his objection to a particular war, to participate in the murder, deceit, and cruelty inherent in war as such.

America has a long record of resistance to conscription, at least in peacetime; that is, we did until the time of the First World War. It surprises me that this opposition became so dormant in the period after the Second World War, and I have been highly encouraged that there is now so much opposition to the draft.

My objection to military conscription includes opposition to the noble sounding idea of universal conscription for social services, even as it has been advocated by many excellent people, including the anthropologist, Margaret Mead. First, I doubt if the government could do a good job of placing all young people in the form of service which would be most useful to them and to their country. I should, of course, like to see it become the custom for young people to serve society for a two-year stint, but I should also like to see it remain a matter of choice. Moreover, I am sure that no American government is likely to pass a Universal Conscription Law without covering the fact that it will send some of the conscripts, willy-nilly, into the army.

During the Vietnamese War there already developed a refusal to accept conscription, and courageous young men were willing to disobey the law openly at the risk of prison, and the stigma that attaches to "draft-dodgers." The government undertook to enforce the draft by proceeding against older men, who courageously advised students to refuse the draft. These men have not acted in secrecy, and they are willing, if necessary, to pay the price for their opposition. They feel that they do not want immunity from the difficult problem of conscription simply by reason of their age. There is, however, a test case, involving Dr.

Benjamin Spock, the famous pediatrician, Rev. William Sloane Coffin, Jr., Chaplain of Yale University, Mitchell Goodman, author, Marcus Raskin, Co-Director of the Institute for Policy Studies, and Michael Ferber, a young Harvard graduate student. The final outcome of this case may be very significant.

Whatever the results, the defendants can morally claim to have outstanding precedents in American history. One was the operation of the Underground Railroad in the Civil War. It was quite illegal to help slaves get to the North and to Canada, but it was a tribute to a magnificent sense of *duty* to violate the law, and the participants are now universally admired. Less heroic, of course, were those who practiced civil disobedience of the Prohibition Law.

Another example to which practitioners of civil disobedience concerning the war in Vietnam can refer is to the decision of the International Court at Nuremberg after the Second World War. This case disallowed the claim of some Germans that they were "simply following orders." The Court ruled, in effect, that there was a type of disobedience which the individual should not only tolerate but practice.

In this country, civil disobedience has most often been connected with either opposition to war, or to racial injustice. There is this difference in the kinds of cases that have been presented. Most of the arrests in racial demonstrations were of men guilty of violating local laws which the demonstrators thought were unconstitutional. In very many cases the Supreme Court has supported that contention. There is, I think, less hope of such a result in the United States vs. Spock et al case, or in the case of the men who have refused induction.

Ethically, however, the same questions underlie all of the cases of so-called civil disobedience in the last few years. I am not a believer in civil disobedience, per se. I criticized disobedience, for instance, during Prohibition, although I thought the law was unworkable. Further, I believe that we presently have too much civil disobedience defended by well-paid, high-powered attorneys. I have also been slow in supporting the non-payment of taxes as a protest against the war on the general ground that everyone could then find it possible to refuse to pay taxes connected with a cause in which he did not believe. Some conservatives, for example, very genuinely object to certain taxes being used for public welfare. Also, the government can collect the taxes by attaching the bank account or income of the derelict taxpayer.

There are, however, men of high character who feel that they must make an effort, even if it is largely symbolic, not to pay taxes for war. This attitude could be justified only as a last resort of protest against a war which they felt was so infamous that they could not live without deducting what they reckoned to be the part of their tax dollar used to support the war in Vietnam. They objected to the conscription of their dollars almost as much as they objected to the conscription of their sons. They can make a case for what they did such as I do not think can be made by those who refuse to pay any federal income tax because of military expenditures. It is definitely the duty of those who protest by withholding taxes not to let their repudiation establish or strengthen a general repudiation of a citizen's duty to pay any income taxes at all because he objects to the Vietnam War and the terrible proportion of our taxes appropriated for armaments (79% in 1967). In this time, it is the general duty of the moral citizen to support higher taxes for essential social services, and to work for the use of tax money for those services rather than armament.

Recently another manifestation of civil disobedience requires much of our attention. It is the widespread student revolt and pressure on the part of students for reforms, both in the University and in general society.

I do not profess to be an authority on education, but there is no doubt that our system requires overhauling from the kindergarten through the University. There is also no doubt that some of the changes must be frankly experimental and in themselves subject to change. Somehow or other, students from elementary schools through the university must be made to feel that they are participants in the course of their own education. At the college and university level, the student body is composed of men considered the right age for the draft, and a great many of them are eligible to vote. They can certainly be considered a very vital part of a university in which the other groups, the faculty and administration, supposedly represent the public interest, whether universities today are directly state controlled, or privately operated institutions. It should be a cause for hope, not despair, that rather suddenly students, or more accurately, a minority of them, have taken as intelligent a view as they have of the problems of curricula and the general governing of their institutions.

Most of the demonstrations can be praised for the objectives sought and the manner in which they are conducted. They are not justified, however, in terms of civil liberties or sound social action when the activist minorities manifest a kind of violent nihilism—especially that evidenced during the Columbia revolt of April and May, 1968. In this revolt, black students seem to have acted with more dignity than white. If the conduct of the more extreme of the latter is considered justified, we can have little to say about possible black mobs in the city. The students themselves did immense harm by their easy appeal to violence, apparently including arson and the outrageous destruction of a professor's life work.

It would be a grave calamity to have to live under a government of men who did these things. Their actions are not justified by the fact that some policemen fought back with inexcusable violence, or that the College Administration was, to put it mildly, very inept in its handling of the situation.

It is very good that America has so successfully found guarantees for civil liberties and civil rights in our Constitution, but the moral case for these rights and liberties is not derived from the Constitution. It is derived from the kind of thinking so well expressed by Thoreau in his *Essay on Civil Disobedience,* which he wrote in opposition to the Mexican War: There come times in life when our conception of our duties may be determined by the conviction that we ought to obey God, rather than man.

We should remember that our great aim is to achieve a world without war. This achievement would pretty well end the need for the kind of civil disobedience that commands so much of our attention today.

# 8

# TOWARD VIOLENCE
# OR NON-VIOLENCE

I want to make it clear that I do not think the solutions I have suggested to the problems we have discussed in this book would create a democratic-socialist utopia, the ideal government I can dream about and hope mankind will someday reach. Our present problem is to consider solutions that have at least a chance of being adopted in a short period of time—before disaster overtakes us. Time is of the essence.

One facet of the overall problem is to get rid of, or at least greatly minimize, the violence which is so large a factor in our modern confusion. Too many reformers and revolutionaries quite sincerely believe, or act as if they believe, that the end justifies the means—any means. This is a doctrine that has been responsible for a great deal of misery, deceit, torture, murder; a doctrine which encourages us to judge our past wars with too little regard for what they have cost us in the deaths of the most coura-

geous and hopeful of our young men, and the intense agony
of civilians.

One of the most serious signs of our times is that after
two World Wars, with their immense destruction, men
seem readier than ever to resort to violence in their personal and public affairs. Violence is no new thing in
public life, but never before has it been so easy for any one
to get hold of extremely dangerous weapons, guns of all
sorts, Molotov cocktails, and immensely more sophisticated
explosives. No one with the slightest imagination can fail
to recognize that a small, determined, and fanatical minority can thus destroy our cities and create horrifying
havoc. What this minority cannot do is create a better life
for those in whose name the violence is used. In America
it can only satisfy a natural, but immensely destructive
passion for revenge. Unquestionably, we must rapidly find
alternatives to violence, and this applies to police brutality
as well as rioting demonstrators.

While it is true that the most significant revolutions—
American, French, Russian and Chinese—were achieved
by violence, one can argue about whether these violent
revolutions were justified by the reforms they brought
about, and whether each one was worth the price it cost
in human suffering. It is also claimed that violence in
these revolutions served as a semi-mystical purgative.

I cannot share this point of view, and cite only one
example: the terrible revolution in Vietnam, an unmiti-
gated evil which affected to some degree all our recent
conduct, not for the best. The war, I believe, has been a
stimulant to domestic crime, to crime in the streets, which
so greatly concerns us. If a man must kill for the sake of

his country's interest, it is asked, why then can't he kill for the sake of his gang or group? If our nation can rain down bombs and napalm indiscriminately on towns and villages in Vietnam, why shouldn't aggrieved, oppressed minorities resort to the violence of guerrilla war in the streets, and this at a time when a small group could practically destroy our cities, and throw our economy into chaos.

We have had enough tragic experience to know what rioting can mean. Rioting, as a planned weapon of wholesale destruction, may indeed destroy the whole established order, but it, and those who use it, will not be building any sort of promised land by this nihilism, and the evidence of our times demonstrates conclusively that destruction does not breed a new and desirable order. That doctrine, sometimes called Castroism, which holds that, first, you have your revolution, and only then do you decide in positive terms what it was for, has worked no triumphs for human society.

Necessarily, I have admitted the role of violence in the great revolutions, and I shall not here try to argue that the satisfactory results of these revolutions might have been achieved by a more evolutionary process. The Indian revolution against England *was* that strange phenomenon —a non-violent revolution, but I cannot say that it, any more than the Russian revolution, put India into the purlieus of utopia.

There is a great cynicism in America, especially among the young, about the effectiveness of the democratic process in achieving a just and fraternal society. I admit that today's cynicism has some justification, but I think it is unnecessarily exaggerated. I am sure that the same factors which produced this situation here have operated in revolutionary countries, thus taking some of the bloom off the notion that revolutionary violence can more or less automatically bring a good society to birth. At best, this kind of violence can break certain "yolks," as Czarism and capitalism did in the USSR. But in the process, this "breaking" produced a brutal, totalitarian State, rather than the people's democracy the revolutionaries had dreamt of.

The amelioration and cure of the Stalinism that rose out of the Russian revolution is now being achieved by an evolutionary process rather than by a resort to guerrilla war. The destruction of the established order in the United States probably *can* be achieved by dedicated violence on the part of a minority of our population, but as with all other revolutions, there will be no guarantee—quite the reverse—of progress toward utopia. This violence has already taken savage forms. For example, during riots there have been incidents of deliberate sniping at firemen who are trying to save lives. Who would like to live under the kind of government achieved by this sort of criminality?

One cannot discuss human conduct simply in terms of the rationality of man, or, on the other hand, accept a full-blown deterministic view, particularly an economic determinism, as the basis of human behavior. There are elements of human irrationality with which we must deal both in ourselves and in society. The ways we make a living and the supremacy of the profit motive in a capitalistic society are tremendously important in influencing human conduct, but are not absolutely determinative. Adam Smith and Karl Marx would probably be equally surprised by the changes in human society since they wrote their great works.

The reasons for the changes have created societies where men and women do not find themselves utterly bound to Calvinist pre-destination *or* to the rigid Marxist interpretation of history. Both forms of determinism are doctrines against which we must contend, conducive as they are to violence. The world we live in now, the world of computers, the whole field of cybernetics, is helping to create a future much less easy to predict than formerly.

Thus, it is a simple fact that we made more progress toward ending the Vietnam horror because of the work of many groups in that direction, who crossed class lines in many unexpected ways, than we did from the "historical" enemy of war, the working class in this country whose official voice is the hawkish AFL-CIO. In the wars through which I have lived, appeals for peace have always been accompanied by more or less extensive drops on the stock market. However, this was not the case when President Johnson first surprised the world by agreeing to at least start negotiations. Stock prices soared on Wall Street.

This is the sort of world in which we live, one in which the working of cause and effect can be better judged from past history than projected in prophecy. But this we know: a great deal can be accomplished by men who will work as hard for a program of non-violent reform as do the dedicated revolutionaries seeking salvation through violence.

# 9

# THE ELECTORAL PROCESS

So far we have been discussing the ends that will result in the good society. The political tools we choose to achieve this end are very important—the means we use necessarily influence the ends.

On the whole, our federal Constitution, with its Bill of Rights, has served as well or better over a longer period of time than any other existing constitution. But I want to discuss some aspects of its provisions for electing government officials, particularly in view of the fact that 1968 saw a renewed interest in the ways we choose a President of the United States—an interest I failed to arouse among the American people in six national campaigns of my own for the Presidency. The examination of this problem has been extended into the whole field of government; the proper balance between the federal, state, and local branches, and how to use, in all areas, a necessary bureaucracy without suffocating under its dead weight. Bureaucracy is not just a problem on the federal level, but in local and state governments. The movement headed by former

Governor of Alabama, George C. Wallace, demonstrates some alarming contradictions. Wallace and his followers call for an end to "big government," an end to the "federal monster" in the name of something they call "states' rights." Many Americans know that this is simply a veil for an essentially racist philosophy. This is not a new tactic. It has been used by other men far greater than the demagogue from Alabama. One thinks of John Calhoun, before the American Civil War, whose "states' rights" doctrines were largely intended to protect the "peculiar institution"—the name he gave to the abomination of chattel slavery.

The campaign year of 1968 brought the question of electing the President to sharp public attention. Events have emphasized the weaknesses in our present policies, but, hearteningly, it was also seen that within the present system the people's voice could be heard, for example, through the work of people involved in the Dump Johnson campaign.

The provisions in our Constitution for electing a President or a Vice President, or for giving the Vice President some measure of usefulness and authority—in addition to his ceremonial duties—are not the wisest ones. The President is an official of tremendous importance in the United States, for whom all the people feel that they vote. Of all public officials, he most arouses the interest of all the people. Yet we cannot vote for him directly, but must express our preferences through the machinery of an electoral college, which makes it possible to elect a President who receives less than a plurality of the popular vote, but a majority in the Electoral College. Three Presidents were thus chosen: John Quincy Adams, Benjamin Harrison, and Rutherford B. Hayes. Our ancestors were extremely fortunate to have fared so well under these minority Presidents.

It has always seemed curious to me that this issue has aroused as little interest as it has in the past. In many speeches I have outlined a plan for the direct election of the President with protection—preferably through a plan of preferential voting—against the possibility that a candidate in a badly divided field will win with only a small plurality vote.

Under President Johnson's administration, the 25th Amendment to the Constitution was adopted clarifying the role of the Vice President in the event of the temporary incapacity of the President, and providing for an orderly Presidential succession in the event the Vice President becomes President.

The 25th Amendment, however, does not touch that undemocratic, and potentially dangerous institution, the Electoral College. At the present time, Congress has an amendment before it which would abolish the Electoral College, and provide for direct elections. Naturally, these proposals should be measured in relation to the principle of one man, one vote. This country needs to vote directly on the basis of the national interest for the one man who represents us all. It will be hard to bring this about because Congress tends to stick to existing election principles. These principles have long outlived their usefulness, for they were created when the Constitution was first written at a time of bargaining and compromise in order to achieve any sort of federal union.

Under the Electoral College system, even in a country devoted to the one man-one vote theory, we can easily have a minority President in case of the failure of any candidate to win enough electoral votes. By throwing the choice of the President into the House, there could be much distasteful maneuvering in terms of the states' presumed interests rather than those of the country as a whole. What applies to the Presidency also applies to the Vice Presidency, but the Vice President is elected by the Senate in case of a deadlock. The Senate would probably complete its task before the House, making it possible for the Vice President to be inaugurated at the proper time. There being no President-elect, it is at least conceivable that the Vice President would then become President.

There are no complications like these for election to the Senate or the House. The principle of one man, one vote, now works more fairly to represent the people than did the original plan of having Senators elected by the state legislatures.

Another important question has been raised by President Johnson. He, among others, has suggested the possibility of electing Congressmen to four-year terms which would coincide with Presidential terms. This plan would go far toward helping to obviate the dangers of an executive-legislative stalemate. There is also the fact that the short term for Congressmen, the long term for Presidents, and the longer term for Senators has encouraged reactionaries to obstruct legislation clearly demanded by a majority of the American people. A classic example of such obstruction concerns gun control legislation, that a majority of the American people wanted, but which was successfully defeated by powerful private interests.

The problem of the democratic election of a President is complicated by the increase in campaign costs. The use of radio and television is now indispensable, and, in general, this is to the good. Whatever their faults, they are at present invaluable sources of information and have helped to expose and correct what has been called the "credibility gap" in the government's own statements, for instance, about the war in Vietnam. The hours of political speculation on television and radio, even when an effort is made to avoid direct propaganda, has a great significance which we have only begun to investigate. Television makes the appearance of candidates and their varying "charismas," their ability to deal on the spot with interviewers and audiences, much more important.

It's my own guess that Abraham Lincoln would not have been elected if, in 1860, he had been compelled to present himself over television, or possibly, due to his very thin voice, even the radio. His angular awkwardness, which Americans have come to cherish in their love for this great man would have counted against him if there had been TV cameras haunting the campaign of 1860.

But set against the unquestioned value of TV and radio the greatest single drawback to its use is the enormous increase of the cost of campaigning. Under our present laws, minority parties are virtually excluded from access to every home, which, theoretically, electronics gives to every candidate. You have to have the money for this, and you cannot get it in any amount comparable to that available for the major party candidates.

Since the major parties are compelled to get money to cover the costs of TV and other forms of modern campaigning, I have marvelled at the relative independence of elected officials to their financial backers. But the situation is thoroughly unhealthy. One hour of prime TV time across the nation now costs far more than either Eugene Debs or I ever had for a whole campaign. To run a successful campaign for the important offices—gubernatorial, senatorial, Presidential—costs more than anyone but the very rich can finance.

As a partial solution to this problem, I have suggested to Congress that holders of TV and radio licenses should be obliged as part of the cost of their licenses to provide X hours of good listening time free from advertising every week for discussion of public issues, and that for a certain number of weeks—let us say four or six—before important elections, time should be given to political discussion by the candidates. Some way may be found to give minor candidates on the ballot a way to share in this time. Various suggestions have been made for the government to limit the costs of campaigning and pay a basic part of it. For a while Senator Russell Long's scheme, under which taxpayers could indicate that one dollar out of their income tax would be paid to a government commission to be divided among the major parties, was considered. No minority party could be considered as a beneficiary unless it had received 5,000,000 votes in the previous election, a near impossibility without this kind of financial support. There were other objections to the plan, which was fortunately abandoned.

Television and radio are pretty well open now to anyone

who has the price, and there are many discussion shows
of varying worth. Difficulties in getting time are now more
financial than ideological, which is a change for the better
from the early days. At the beginning of extensive radio
communication, I recall being barred from speaking on
several occasions because the radio authorities wanted
me to delete parts of my speeches. On principle I refused.
In later years I was treated rather better by radio and
television. They took care, however, to see that I had no
regular place on any of the panels for discussion of public
issues. After the Second World War, I was told by a very
high network official that they couldn't possibly have me
appear on a regular basis because it would have offended
too many of their advertisers.

After the disgraceful exhibition in Chicago during the
summer of 1968 at the Democratic Convention, the national nominating conventions have received the criticism
they have deserved for a long time. They have been
assailed as undemocratic circuses in which really important questions could only be buried in verbiage. 1968
bore out this contention, at least in large part. The successful Republican and Democratic nominees had done
badly in public opinion polls, but the "regular organization" in each party pushed them through—this, in spite
of the fact, that on such crucial issues as Vietnam there
was little to choose between them. Indeed, the major
debates occurred within the parties, not, as they should,
between them. There were some hopeful signs, however,
particularly the ending of the "unit rule" at Democratic
conventions.

Most public discussion involves election to the legislative and executive branches of the government, but in many states, there are also elections to the judicial branch, and in some states there is machinery for appointments that makes them desirable plums for one or other of the major parties. Candidates are expected to contribute to the party which nominated them. How they are elected or appointed is a very important factor in the serious problem of the administration of justice at all levels.

When I lived in slum areas in New York, I listened to more complaints from the poor about the administration of justice than about anything else. Civil suits in New York State often take from four to six years to come to trial. The cost of suits and the difficulty of prosecuting even a criminal case means that many cases that should be heard are never brought to the courts. New York has tried to alleviate this condition by provisions calling for the appointment of another 125 judges. But these provisions leave a great deal to be desired. They lack the safeguards to keep the judgeships from being plums provided by wheeling-dealing politicians. One result of the inadequate administration of justice is that no plan to battle poverty will be at all adequate that does not deal with the cost of obtaining justice. Over and over a poor man is confined indefinitely in prison because he cannot afford bail, which the most undesirable characters can get if they have the price.

Beside fairer methods of electing officials, there is a need for ways of imposing better self-discipline on our legislators. Hypocrisy is rampant in this area, from the local to the federal level. That Congressman-rogue, Adam Clayton Powell, succinctly summed up a cynical attitude, but one that is close to the truth. He was described as only angering his colleagues in the House when, confronted with various charges of misconduct, he stated: "I haven't done anything more than any other Congressmen," and added that "nor by the grace of God, do I intend to do anything *less*."

We must intensify controls over the flagrant and often dishonest lobbying on behalf of special interests. Alternatively, we must continue to encourage the sort of lobbying that has a very valid place in our system; that is, lobbying on behalf of what has been accurately called the public interest. For instance, the exemplary efforts of Ralph Nader.

Finally, I believe that a democracy, especially in a country as large as the United States, needs electoral parties that represent the people. The nature of these parties depends, in the last analysis, on the people—their education and their will to decency and freedom. Whatever our level of achievement in this area, I do not think that our present system can be replaced by any other of the presently available forms. A two-party system has many advantages so long as each party remains the servant of the issues and not vice-versa.

I feel strongly about the serious need for constructive reevaluation of our political machinery, always keeping in mind the fact that the basic structure is good. It is not enough to say, as we criticize our present party system, "Let's form our own party." This should always be a possibility, but the decision to form another party should only be made with great care.

We live in a world where *considered* choice is necessary, and it is imperative to remember that the improvements we want in our very substantial imperfections are not to be found in nihilist doctrines or in a political dictatorship of either the right or the left.

# 10

## POLITICAL ACTION, 1968

In discussing the very grave issues of this time I have so far said little about the great political ideologies and their application to our present political situation. I should expect to be asked, I suppose, whether I am still a democratic socialist, or to hear again oft-repeated comment that I "must be very happy now because the Socialist Party platforms on which you ran were so largely taken up by Democrats and Republicans."

"Franklin D. Roosevelt carried out most of the immediate demands of your programs," I am very frequently told. Just as frequently, I suggest that some of those demands were carried out on a stretcher, and I recall incidents which support this view. I remember he compared himself to a lifeguard, who, after bringing a drowning woman to shore, gets his face slapped for pulling her hair. On one occasion Roosevelt expressed his wrath to me over some hostile Chamber of Commerce resolutions, and what seemed to be his anger with the whole American business community for its failure to recognize that the

Roosevelt Administration had actually *saved* capitalism.

At the beginning of his first administration, he rejected our proposals for radical banking reforms, and throughout his administration he answered our pleas for adequate federal relief for sharecroppers and other agricultural workers with the excuse that no one could do much with the present generation of Southern landlords.

Franklin D. Roosevelt became neither an anarchist, a communist, or a democratic-socialist. At least until World War II, these ideologies were, in a broad sense, representative of the major divisions on the left.

Anarchy seemed to have died out even before World War II. In the 1960's, however, it has been revised by certain elements of the New Left, but in ways which its original proponents would find strange. This was borne out at the 1968 convention of anarchists in Italy when Daniel Cohn-Bendit, the leader of the 1968 student uprisings at the Sorbonne, and invited as an honored guest to the convention, roundly denounced the assembled anarchists, and was similarly denounced himself.

Communism and democratic-socialism as political movements continue to exert great influence, but not as pure ideologies. I, emphatically, am still a democratic-socialist, which means that I believe in a far more equitable distribution of the Gross National Product than we have, and an extension of social ownership to achieve that end. I believe in democracy, and in the increase of democratic planning in both America and the world, where the growth in population and our remarkable advances in technology have made such planning both more necessary and more difficult to achieve. I continue to feel that the adoption of the basic principles of democratic socialism is essential, but in the light of events of the last twenty years we now know that their adoption, or the adoption of any other formal ideology, will not automatically resolve particular issues. Deep quarrels between democratic-socialists on these issues necessarily prove this assertion.

Developments since the first World War, and especially since World War II, have not fulfilled my dream that democratic-socialism would dramatically create conspicuously successful communities. Democratic-socialism, in countries where it has achieved some political power, has not been completely successful in differentiating itself from welfare state capitalism. But I wish to repeat my belief that even the *relative* successes of this ideology have been vastly superior to the achievements growing out of authoritarian answers to the problems we have discussed, whether they be of the right or the left, the answers of a Hitler, a Franco or a Stalin.

Swedish Social Democrats have been reelected in 1968 to lead a government they have administered with great imagination, skill, and courage for the last thirty-six years. Thanks largely to young voters, they achieved the first full majority since 1940, gaining seats from both the right and the extreme left. All of this was, of course, heartening to me, but I noted that the democratic-socialist gains came on the basis of particular issues such as Swedish abhorrence of the recent Russian invasion of Czechoslovakia, and opposition to the American involvement in Vietnam, etc., rather than from strict ideological concerns. There is an analogy in the history of the American Socialist Party (as, of course, there is in the history of all democratic-socialist parties.) During the 1930's, many members of our party went over to the New Deal, to work in the Democratic Party. It was interesting that men in about equal numbers from both the left and the right wings of our party joined this effort. Some of them said that there was no hope outside of their own Marxist ideology, but that they had to leave the Socialist Party because it did not indicate the best way to achieve the specific objectives which they sought!

Having said all this, my belief has not changed that such democratic communities as I have sought for through the whole of my adult political life can never be achieved through communism or any other authoritarian solution.

Communism itself, fortunately, is no longer the monolithic force it was under Stalin, and it shows important signs of an evolution toward greater freedom and respect for the individual. The communist world has its own sharp differences, as in September, 1968, even *Pravda* was forced to admit regretfully. Thus one thinks of the tensions among the Communist regimes of Russia, China, Cuba, Czechoslovakia, or Yugoslavia. However, we cannot forget that even now *all* communist parties are to a large degree still totalitarian and dictatorial, and possess a kind of public ethic which permits the good of each party to be the final determinant of right or wrong. The brutal intervention of the USSR in Czechoslovakia in August, 1968 is only the latest example of this attitude, particularly the Russians' masking of their national "self-interests" with the rationale that they intervened (according to Tass) "to save socialism."

The foregoing paragraphs indicate why I have concentrated less, in this book, on broad ideological questions than on particular ones. As I approach the end of my life, my deepest concern involves the end of war, all war, and the establishment of good relationships among all races. I feel that there is no great ideology, however useful it may be on specific issues, which will solve these problems alone. *We have been forced to deal with particulars* in searching for solutions, and to do so without the luxury of indulging in parochial quarrels or personal motives, however noble or self-sacrificing. We live, moreover, in a time when the debates of the first forty years of this century have become less and less relevant to the young people searching for answers in the 1960's. Many commentators have remarked on the differences between the radicals of the 1930's and the 1960's. Discussing the politics of 1968, one would be foolish, as well as remiss, in not commenting on these differences.

The communists went very far in believing that the end justifies the means, whereas many New Left activists believe that the means *determine* the ends, and that, today, the means that will achieve useful social changes require a greater or lesser degree of violence including murder. They reject political action by decrying its usefulness. They harp on the failures of parliamentary democracy to solve discrimination against Negroes even as they seem oblivious of the fact that violent demonstrations have contributed more toward magnifying a white backlash against peaceful reforms than largely non-violent demonstrations have at least brought about on paper.

In 1968, this apotheosis of violence had not yet prevented a use for politics among both black and white activists. At the same time, they found no place for their politics or a really satisfactory home in any of the major parties in the United States or elsewhere. Nevertheless, they got results of importance. For instance, it was largely through their work that Lyndon B. Johnson was persuaded not to run for a second term.

1968 represented an important turning point in American history, for both good and terrifying reasons. Never before had there been so much intelligent knowledge of our problems. At few times in our history had the young been so courageous and encouraged more hope. They performed an extraordinary service under the leadership of such men as Allard Lowenstein in carrying through the Dump Johnson Movement. That movement, at first very small, finally persuaded one Senator, Eugene J. McCarthy of Minnesota, to seek the Democratic nomination for the Presidency, a nomination which he was volubly assured he could not get. McCarthy's effort in the New Hampshire primary encouraged Senator Robert F. Kennedy to change his mind about running, and after Kennedy's tragic assassination, Senator George McGovern of South Dakota, shortly before the Democratic convention, attempted to carry on as Senator Kennedy's unofficial successor.

These efforts culminated in defeat of their candidates at the Democratic convention, a riotous gathering controlled by Mayor Daley of Chicago and his police. Naturally, this result was profoundly disappointing to the young, many of whom, I am afraid, turned to a basically nihilist philosophy. I shared their profound disappointment in the defeat of Senator McCarthy. I also felt disappointed that my old friend, Hubert H. Humphrey, once a sincere and influential liberal, was so opportunistically tied to the banner of what he sometimes called the Johnson-Humphrey Administration. But disappointing as the results of the Democratic Convention were, the Democratic rebels and their independent friends had earlier succeeded by their ardor and tactics, not only in forcing President Johnson's retirement, but in gaining more recognition from him of the possibility for successful negotiations in Vietnam than he had formerly admitted. It was these rebels, too, who stimulated public criticism of the Electoral College system, of dangerous, undemocratic procedures in national nominating conventions, and of the constitutional method of electing a President. It was a great achievement, but unfortunately not great enough at a moment in history when time is of the essence and we must end all war in Southeast Asia and provide workable alternatives to the guerrilla war activities of some seekers of racial justice.

It is significant, however, that the relatively small-sized minorities have accomplished as much as they have in the brief period since the decline of Johnson's popularity. This gain was seriously offset by the progress of Governor George Wallace's racist campaign, which seemed to appeal to the American masses in a strikingly disturbing degree. He seemed to have proved that what might be described as the lower middle classes and many of the white poor are more concerned about state's rights and the control of crime by contempt for civil liberties than we had anticipated. These issues are for them and with Governor Wallace, a facade for racism. It is in this area that a great job of education must be done, not only by eloquent speech of which we have had much but by a convincing demonstration of the value of even our imperfect civil rights and social security laws.

Unfortunately, there is a revival among many on the New Left of the thought that the worse things get, the sooner they can have their revolution—an idea that should have been refuted by the history of the Nazi movement in Germany. Meanwhile, in the years ahead, we must keep up the struggle to influence the soundest American ideals. And we must not underestimate the importance of congressional elections. To be effective I think it necessary to get a much more viable coalition of those deeply concerned for minority rights, civil liberties, social legislation, than the present radical parties of protest provide.

### November 6, 1968

I write on the day following a very close national election. It now appears that this country has averted what might have been a constitutional crisis of the first order. The candidacy of George Wallace very nearly brought the election of the President into the House of Representatives. We cannot, as I indicated in the chapter on The Electoral Process, afford the dangerous luxury of an Electoral College system.

It is an entirely proper use of the word to say that 1968 has been an extraordinary year. It was marked by the assassinations of the Reverend Martin Luther King and Robert F. Kennedy, by extensive riots in the streets of the cities of the world, and by an outspoken, world-wide advocacy of violent revolution.

The appearance, in America, of an evil demagogue,

George Wallace, inspired what was more than a white "backlash." His American Independent Party succeeded in getting on the ballot in all of the fifty states. I can testify through personal experience to the difficulty and expense of achieving that goal.

Happily, George Wallace did not do as well in the election as his supporters hoped, and his opponents feared. He received the electoral votes of only five states, thus winning, on a proportional basis, very few more votes than Strom Thurmond, an advocate of Richard Nixon in 1968, when he ran for the States Rights Party in 1948. But Wallace's strength in what are generally regarded as lower white working class neighborhoods in the North cannot be ignored. One of the chief tasks we face is to note carefully that poor whites, as well as poor blacks, are alienated from some of the common assumptions of middle and upper class Americans concerning "The Affluent Society." The results of the election only re-emphasize the fact that poverty and unhappiness have no relation to color.

Shortly before the election, President Johnson announced that this nation was going to stop the bombing of North Vietnam, and offered to negotiate with the National Liberation Front of North Vietnam. It was a long overdue step, and at the time of this writing the eventual results, for good or bad, remain in question. What is not in doubt, as readers of this book should know, is that the cessation of the bombing, and the recognition of the National Liberation Front, should have been attempted months ago. I can only hope that the move toward peace started in the fall of 1968 brings peace to the tortured country of Vietnam.

President-Elect Richard M. Nixon will assume office with a Congress, both in the Senate and the House, formally opposed to the party he represents. He has inherited a costly and brutal war. He will become President of a nation in which, increasingly, the voices of violence are heard more often than the voices of reconciliation.

Will there be interracial fraternity, or war? Will there be economic justice? Can this country help to build a world without war? I believe these goals can be achieved, and I have written this book in the belief that our younger generation will contribute mightily toward their achievement.

# EPILOGUE:

I have come to the end of this short book well aware that it has pointed to no single or simple road marking the way to a shiny utopia. But I hope I have suggested some valid ways to move, and some of the methods we should employ.

Crude as our democracy is, and has been, I have far more confidence in it than in the new nihilism, or dictatorship of the right or the left. But our democracy must be improved, and the young of this country and the world are our only hope.

I should like to end this book by printing a letter I wrote to the Socialist Party convention in July, 1968. I dictated the letter from a hospital bed, convinced that it was to be my last letter. Happily, the expectation was refuted, but I quote from this letter, reminding you that what I urged on my fellow Socialists, I urge on you, and that the thanks I give to my fellow Socialists, go in my mind and heart to all who have worked in the past, and will work in the future, to end war, and establish a society based on social justice and fraternity.

"I want to begin by saying that we have been all too ready to throw in our hand, too ready simply to bemoan the state of our society in the world. We have too often written ourselves off as being unable to deal nationally with the paramount problem of violence in this country we love, and in a world apparently dedicated to the use of its tremendous scientific power for its own destruction. We do not have to remind ourselves that there is madness about, but we may have to remind ourselves that there is also more to be said than that we are mad.

"More than ever, as a world population once un-dreamed of, we have to be able physically to cooperate for life, rather than death. With all our tremendous mistakes and those of our ancestors, we have done enough to know that we are not damned to breed ourselves to death, or to exhaust actual or potential food supplies in the earth or in the waters of the earth. We *can* reverse the processes of air and water pollution. The question, we know, in these and other matters, is not, *can we,* but, *will we* save ourselves?

"Not for a minute do we need to assume that the human race is irrevocably damned. With this in mind, I find much satisfaction in remembering that the Scandinavians, who have achieved the most intelligent form of social institutions, are the descendants of the wild and cruel Vikings. Repeatedly I remind myself that we have improved on the stupidities and cruelties of 19th-century education, and that, in the United States, for instance, despite some ghastly problems, we were able, if imperfectly, to educate into one nation a host of children from different nations.

"The outstanding difficulty is that man who is so often equipped with great courage, loyalty and devotion to ideals has so often found those ideals unworthy of his devotion. One of the things that we Socialists have always sought to achieve for ourselves and to cultivate in others is a sense of joyous responsibility for ourselves and the world. Men of all races and countries are capable of marvelous loyalty and devotion to their nations. The number of lives saved in the business of saving others is conspicuous and is not to be entirely explained by a simple lust for a certain kind of fame.

"As you know, I have many times spoken caustically as I have worked to correct imperfections in our nation and its institutions, and I have had little but contempt for jingoistic nationalism. This is not because nationalism, over and over, has not brought forth aspects worthy of an ultimate devotion, but because often these aspects have been too strictly limited to one nation, class or group. It is not impossible for us (particularly Socialists) to set up an economic and material structure which will permit us to coexist as New Yorkers, Chicagoans, or even Marionites.

"Patience and friendship can be learned. The task will require a degree of intelligence and a capacity for elementary fraternity which we, of course, have not manifested as we should. But is it impossible to do so? I do not think so. If we are to continue to exist, we must find ways to make our dreams of fraternity more than dreams.

"I have not been talking about an impossible utopia when I continue to say that this world can be motivated and structured in such a way as to achieve a world without war—a world to end the madness which continues to condemn children everywhere to hatred, starvation, disease. The tactics of this great struggle for such a world need continual and fresh evaluation. There is no rigid ideology to insure its achievement. But we have the courage, high hopes and abilities to see that it is done.

"I have no yearning for the immortality of my race, but I do have enough hope to want a return ticket in fifty years or so to see how well you have done. I speak, as you have heard me speak many times, as one of the most fortunate of men—especially as I have had you as comrades."

## DATE DUE

| | | | |
|---|---|---|---|
| FEB 18 1982 | | | |
| | | | |
| MAR 17 1983 | | | |
| SEP 19 1990 | | | |
| | | | |
| | | | |
| | | | |
| | | | |
| | | | |
| | | | |
| | | | |
| | | | |
| | | | |
| | | | |
| | | | |
| | | | |